Descartes' Loneliness

ALLEN GROSSMAN

Descartes' Loneliness

A NEW DIRECTIONS
PAPERBOOK ORIGINAL

ACKNOWLEDGMENTS

"A Long Romance" first appeared in *The Boston Review.* "Treason," "A Kiss for You," "Shopfitters," "The Caedmon Room,"and "A Gust of Wind," first appeared in *New Ohio Review.*

Photograph "Finesse, August 1957" on p. 42 © British Vogue/The Condé Nast Publications.

Book design by Sylvia Frezzolini Severance
Manufactured in the United States of America
New Directions Books are printed on acid-free paper.
First published as a New Directions Paperbook Original (NDP1093) in 2007
Published simultaneously in Canada by Penguin Books Canada Limited

Library of Congress Cataloging-in-Publication Data

Grossman, Allen R., 1932-
  Descartes' loneliness / Allen Grossman.
    p. cm.
  "A New Directions paperbook original"—T.p. verso.
  ISBN 978-0-8112-1711-8 (pbk. : acid-free paper)
  I. Title.

PS3557.R67D47 2007
811'.54—dc22
                                        2007026896

SECOND PRINTING

New Directions Books are published for James Laughlin
by New Directions Publishing Corporation
80 Eighth Avenue, New York, NY 10011

CONTENTS

FOUR

FIVE

Descartes' Loneliness

ONE

DESCARTES' LONELINESS

Toward evening, the natural light becomes
intelligent and answers, without demur:
"Be assured! You are not alone. . . ."
But in fact, toward evening, I am not
convinced there *is* any other except myself
to whom existence *necessarily* pertains.
I also interrogate myself to discover
whether I *myself* possess any power
by which I can bring it about that I
who now am shall exist another moment.

Because I am mostly a thinking thing
and because this precise question can only
be from that thoughtful part of myself,
if such a power did reside within me
I should, I am sure, be conscious of it. . . .
But I am conscious of no such power.
And yet, if I myself cannot be
the cause of that assurance, surely
it is necessary to conclude that
I am not alone in the world. There is

some other who is the cause of that idea.
But if, at last, no such other can be
found toward evening, do I really have
sufficient assurance of the existence
of any other being at all? For,
after a most careful search, I have been
unable to discover the *ground* of that
conviction—unless it be imagined a lonely
workman on a dizzy scaffold unfolds
a sign at evening and puts his mark to it.

SHIPFITTERS

It's a matter of concern to me that Leonardo's
angels—who are so beautiful—are inadequately
provided with wings by the curious master.
Surely Leonardo knew they couldn't arrive here
to pray, or point, or weep, or at the end
save themselves from fire, by the means depicted.

It is also a matter of concern to me that Midge Berger,
wife of Ben Berger who owned the Mpls. Lakers,
played a good game of golf despite a tic
over her left eye (which raised her handicap),
and that Ben, a short man, liked to be photographed
next to George Mikan (6'3") whom he hired for the purpose.

Midge was best friend of Beatrice, my mother.
Both girls are dead now. But it's still a matter of
concern to me that Ben and Midge went to China
in 1951 and that Midge carried back in her lap
(28 hours, PAN AM) a model river boat, a "junk,"
as a present for Beatrice, empress of Mpls.

and its streams. The boat was made by learned felons
in Nanking prison on the Yangzte, all dead,
but in their time they knew *how to make a boat.*
They would have been loftsmen, welders, riveters,
anglesmiths, flange turners and the like. Look how
the hull, the spars, the sails, etc., are clearly right!

They were competent men. They knew how boats work.
I said to myself: "That will be my death-ship,

when it comes time."—And *now* the wind rises.
The tide is at the flood. The great green sails set
downstream, toward the harbor busy with trade.
The winds shift offshore.—Friend, be thou assured!

WASH DAY

July, 1947, Gibbon, Minn.

Soiled thoughts heap up
like rags in a basket.
Time to do a wash.
The weather's right,
bright and windy.
A quick-dry day.

First, soap. Not store-bought.
But stone-hard pig fat
and lye mixed with
oatmeal in a pail.
Then hacked with a knife
into Lux-like flakes.

Then the washer, gas-powered.
Hard to start in the
kitchen, but too heavy
to lug outside.
"*Fumes!*" (There's
a word for you!)

The blue-enameled kitchen
stove burns corncobs
gnawed clean by pigs.
After the pigs have done
their damnedest,
the cobs burn hot.

Water. Well-water
is real cold.

No stove, pigs or not,
is hot enough to bring
well-water to blood heat.
For that you need a heart.

In the root cellar
beneath the kitchen
potatoes sprout
dead white—
because there's
no light.

Outside, on wash day, are
two galvanized steel tubs
for rinsing in the lovely air.
Rinse Tub One: rainwater, sheer joy.
Rinse Tub Two: the blueing,
too cold to be true.

Then, everything dries on the line
in the winds of July.
What dries first?
Handkerchiefs and lady's underwear.
What dries last?
The farmer's overalls

heavy with desire.
On the bib,
where the heart beats,
his everlasting snuff tin
has inscribed an unwashable
perfect circle forever.

At noon, the naked truth descends
offering her stunning breasts.
Also here comes the prophet
Amos, with something in hand.
In fact, a basket of summer fruit.
Ch. 8, vss. 1, 2. (Check it out.)

A DAY'S WORK

Buying a grave, choosing a mother.
August again. Morning. Wisdom.
Dreams: I am choosing a mother
in the future, before this time.
And in the afternoon, buying a grave.
—There she is. Pre-war.

Bobbed hair conceals
ears. Starched white shirt. (Sleeves
rolled up with fierce intent.)
Hands in pockets of a straight skirt
of heavy material. She is looking
at the ground.

This happened once,
long ago.
As for the rest:
burn me and make my
grave in the stream and the stream-
bed of a fiery brook.

THE CAEDMON ROOM

Upstairs, one floor below the Opera House
(top floor of the building), is the Caedmon
room—a library of sorts. The Caedmon room
was empty of readers most of the time.
When the last reader left and closed the door,
I locked it and moved in for life. Right now,
I am writing this in the Caedmon room.
Caedmon was an illiterate, seventh-century
British peasant to whom one night a lady
appeared in a dream. She said to him, speaking
in her own language, "Caedmon! Sing me something!"
And he did just that. What he sang, in *his*
own language, was consequential—because
he did not learn the art of poetry
from men, but from God. For that reason,
he could not compose a trivial poem,
but what is right and fitting for a lady
who wants a song. These are the words he sang:
"Now praise the empty sky where no words are."
This was Caedmon's song. Caedmon's voice is sweet.
In the Caedmon room shelves groan under the
weight of his eloquent blank pages, histories
of a sweet world in which we are not found.
Caedmon turned each page, page after page
until the last page—on which is written:
"To the one who conquers, I give the morning star."

WINTER AT THE SEASHORE

"Nightfall.
Journey's end.

Having come this far,
we are at the shore.

Look up. Over there!
That high tower

is mind.
Look down.

This world below us
is a furious coast.

Think back over
the straightening

of the seasons. Remember!
Sowing, then burgeoning,

then seed-fall. And now
this harvest:

winter
wheat."

"Allen, what is that flail
on your shoulder?

What is it for?"
"It's the oar

that brought us
to this night

and furious coast,
among winds."

"Look! That high tower
strews signals."

"Listen! Zeus, the counsellor,
decrees snow."

TIMOR MORTIS, INC.,
A SWITCHBOARD MEMORY

(Chicago, 1928)

The business plan of Timor Mortis, Inc.,
required reconstruction of its switchboard.
As soon as it was completed, Beatrice
appeared from her grave to man a position.
Outgoing—from below, local—requires
that she reach down, pull up a plug, and then
throw the plug into a socket above
her head, so that she can say to anyone,
with a number, a long way off: "It's time."
Incoming—from above, afar—requires
that she reach up over her head, grab a
plug, and throw it into a socket with
the corresponding number beneath her knees.
"Somebody is calling, calling, calling. . . . "

CITY OF DAVID

Jerusalem is a grave of poets. Name
two who are buried there:
the poet Dennis Silk is buried there.
He lived with a dressmaker's dummy,
in a cave, on the Hill of Evil
Counsel due south of Zion Mount.
She bore him children
after her kind.—In any case, whatever
she gave birth to did not live.
Famous Amichai, also a poet,
is buried there. From his apartment on
the eastern slope you can see
a gate of the City, called David's Gate.
In '48, on a beach at Tel Aviv,
the poet Amichai held a dying soldier
in his arms. The soldier whispered—:
"Shelley." And then he died.
Poets built Jerusalem. Therefore,
poets have a duty to destroy
Jerusalem. If I forget thee,
the world will be better off.
The tree a cat can get up into,
a cat can get down from by itself.

TWO

THE INVENTION OF NIGHT

venit Hesperus, ite capellae

evening comes, go home goats

Virgil, *Eclogue X*

In the Allerton Hotel, downtown Chicago,
fifty-three years ago, I opened a book and heard
Virgil's pastoralist for the first time.
He was mourning the loss of his friends
gone off with one another, but now
themselves lost. I communed then
with Arethusa, a fountain of that place.
From a room down the hall, on the left,
I heard the cry of a man in pain. . . .

On April 21, 1951, General MacArthur
was parading up Michigan Avenue,
ordered home from Korea by President Truman
for threatening use of nuclear weapons.
People in Chicago greeted MacArthur's
boast with flowers and music. But Truman said,
"General MacArthur is fighting the wrong war."
Paper flowers floated upward into the sun.
Arcadian music was heard on the 23rd floor.

Song is extreme work. Help me, river sister!
It's getting dark. Hey, sweet water! Flow fresh
through ocean's salt. Give me some words for him
I love, so he can give words to someone else.
Start love's gift once more:—WORDS FOR ANOTHER.
So everybody will have something to give someone.
If not, I'll drown you in oceans of salt tears.

Then you'll be indistinguishable from tears.
This is Arcadia. In Arcadia,

sweetheart, everyone hears songs and sings back.
Right now, however, my soldier sits alone
like an animal. He has no gift to give.
"Where are you, sister, word-giver—shining
among what wander-roots, what wet shadows?
Unvisitable source, kiss my mourning man.
Arethusa, kiss my wordless animal
on his mountain, stone-alone, standing around.
Arethusa, where are you?"—"Allen, I am

underground among streams. Here knowledge is."
—That's what she says. *But who knows* where she's gone?
There's Upilio coming up the avenue.
He eats acorns and dirt. He doesn't know.
Here come shepherds, pig-keepers, ploughmen, etc.
And Sylvanus—glorious, mute, and slow
with the grandeur of quaking lillies on his brow
and fennel. After him Arcadia's god who sings,
"Love is strong as death and as indifferent and cruel."

Through the darkening air (*vesper adest*)
I hear my soldier talking to me
from his stone—one stone among all the
stones, but which stone it is I do not know.
What does he say? "Death is an imperceptible
deepening of solitude. I wish I were
still one of you. But an insane love of
war compells me. Tell my story, Arcadians.
Only Arcadians by their art remember

the magnificent graves of the human heart.
She who is lost in the dark is ever fair,
wherever she may be. I hear her sing,
I feel her breath. Love is as strong as death,
but no stronger. Love conquers all but one
last wonder—the limit of the work—oblivion."
That room in the Allerton (23rd floor) had
four walls, thirteen wall surfaces, and one window.
Under the window was a radiator.

Along the wall, a bed on which I lie down.
Opposite the one window, at the other
end of the room, behind my head, is the door.
In sleep, on that bed, something happened to me,
and now it returns again: a dream of the lighters
and the lightermen. Night and day, the lighter -
men ferry crowds of men and women through
an enormous surf out into open ocean.
"Why is death in Arcadia?" the men and women cry.

And the lightermen answer: "No death, no song."
Again, I hear a groan down the hall, on the left.
I get the number, call it, and ask my question,
"What might it mean to take your word to heart?"
And the groaner down the hall answers me:
"What do you want this time, fucker . . . !
What city do YOU live in? Under what
stone? Here we howl and it means nothing."
—So I lie down again, and dream the dream

of the lighter and the lightermen who
ferry wanderers through the surf and out
to a schooner. There it is, luffing offshore,

rigged for the open ocean—whereon looms
the great seafarer, OBLIVION.
—Now follows, Arcadians, invention of night:
There is a tree that grows fast, hour by hour.
At noon, the tree casts a shade. Then deep shade.
Then darkness wounds. After that, kills. What kills?

The darkness under a fast growing tree.

THE LENDING LIBRARY

(Beatrice reads the Gospels)

At her Lending Library on Lake Street, Mpls.,
mother Beatrice rented out books to ladies.
But she read them first. That way she knew whether
there *was not*, or (preferably) *was*, anything
"disgraceful" in them. (There were two kinds of ladies.)
The result was mother owned the second vol.
of many novels (e.g., Scott's *Ivanhoe*).

The first vol. frequently was not returned.
(That's why I know a lot about how things come out
and don't know much about how they begin.)
But mother Beatrice ("Bea" for short) *never read*
one book she owned—it was not to be loaned
or sold—until Xmas ('43). A voice said:
"Bea, now read that one!" And she does.

"Allen, how things looked in the heart of Jesus
I don't know and, frankly, don't want to know.
But I do know *now* that only those souls stirred
by the question of their *existence* can answer
the claim he makes—But, Allen, who does know?
To whose sentences can we say, '*Yes! That's true.*'
And thereby add to the wonder of it *belief.*"

Snow was falling. And that same voice—
maddening, relentless, pornographic—sings
"Silent Night," but doesn't stop at "heavenly peace."
It starts over—again, and again, and again.
At last, the ladies' favorite.
It's about the "babe" who added to the wonder
of it all *belief.*—Three days of that song drives

Beatrice crazy. She gathers up her books-for-rent,
locks the door and says: "Let the ladies *buy* books."
And Bea's voice was heard, despite the singing,
far across the gentile lake by an itinerant master,
Thoreau, who rested on the other shore,
in Minnesota, and caught the cold that killed him.
—There's no Lending Library on Lake St. any more.

How, then, learn the way anything begins,
remembering, as we do, nothing? *What book*
will tell? Certainly not this one. *You* take
the question to heart! I do but write the wonder
and by these poems solicit belief.
There is a road by which we came this far.
There is another by which we must depart.

YOU WILL BE WRAPPED IN SILK

"And how do you merit to live so long?"
—Because I know there is need to consider.

At my birth someone said, "He will be wrapped
in silk." And now the guests are arriving.

The meaning of the prophecy (which they know)
 has drawn them here at the appointed time

for the reason that something is coming to pass
that could not come to pass except for me.

I am the man of whom it was said,
"He will be wrapped in silk." What could

not come to pass except for me? A wedding.
Now the many women, daughters and wives,

arrive at the wedding as I lie asleep on
an embroidered couch, a very short man

and hard to see. They come on a winter
evening to the wedding—wives and elegant

daughters come in from the outside, talking
among themselves, snow glittering in their hair,

and they drop veil after veil on the embroidered couch,
revealing their fine dresses and their jewels,

veil after veil of silk, veil after veil,
until I am completely covered with silk.

A LONG ROMANCE

Whatever that nameless sage, the Mind, utters
in our oldest voices . . . whatever the poem
of Mind keeps on saying, weariless, beyond
my death, or any death . . . and is always
saying—sleepless, even in sleep—to this
hearer and also to every other one . . .
is Wisdom of *our* kind, mortal—*finesse.*
The poem of Mind is for the one hearer,
but is heard the same by anyone who
may, or may not, say it to another.
It is not many lights. It's one long *durée*
of light from noon backward to the hour before
dawn when it's still too dark to say
"Look! Look, my dear, it's snowing in the light."

This beach is strewn with stones. Which is *my* stone?
There *must* be something permanently actual—
eternity, or chaos, or night—something
that moves without being moved. God is an
idea like my sister. But I don't
have a sister—not even a dumb sister.
I don't have a god either—not even a
dumb god. But there is Mind in every
human being, conscious of thinking and
good at it—*aware* in a way that exceeds
any wakefulness the prophets know about.
What does Mind say? "Menstrual fluids are
set in motion by sperm, as earth by seed. . . ."
In any case, nothing I can't understand.

Glimpse, glimpse, glimpse, glimpse, glimpse.
So begins the long romance of instruction.
The snow has fallen all day and heaps up.
The day brightens. The snow dries in the field.
How will it end, now that the end comes on?
The nurse and that other boy in the picture
wander towards the city. The sun is on it . . .
glimpse, glimpse, glimpse, glimpse, glimpse.
The boy has found his stone on the bright beach
strewn with stones. Look! He puts it in his mouth.
Kiss him! Kiss him! Kiss him! Let the stone pass
from his mouth to your open mouth.
Shazam! "The divine literatus comes"
and the winds of heaven blow the great ship home.

YOU HAVE BEAUTIFUL HAIR, IRENE

You have beautiful hair, Irene.
Wisteria on many trees.

At the point of death
the world and the human

world coincide—
a furnished room.

You ask me,"What is
that you carry on

your shoulder, Allen?
Is it a winnowing fan?"

"No! Irene, it is an oar.
Make your hair

a rope. Open the window
and lean out."

I AM THAT I AM

Better a deceiving god than no god at all.
This is experience in a certain mind
—not any mind—but one specific mind
with a particular history *like* yours
or mine, but other than yours and mine
—distinct, utterly unknown to both of us,
entirely other, and yet of the same kind
as your mind, or my mind, or any other.

Here we meet who are otherwise nothing
to one another, neither brother nor friend. . . .
Our minds wander off.—Look! This piece of wax
has not yet lost all taste of its honey.
It retains some odor of the wild flowers
from which it has been gathered by the bee.
It is hard. It is cold. It emits a sound
when stricken. It may be any shape.

But it remains still the same piece of wax.
No one denies that. And I perceive it.
It is *not accidental* to the mind
to be united to the body. Yet how
prone to errors my mind is. If I had
not now looked out the window and seen
a human being going by in the street,
I would not believe it emits a sound

when stricken. Yet I am. I exist. I have
a body which can act and also suffer.
As your highness is so clear-seeing, there

is no concealing anything from you.
—You are not one of those who never philosophize.
The piece of wax is moved toward the fire.
But the piece of wax remains, because
this wax is not perceived except by mind.

But my essence consists wholly in being
a thinking *thing*. Right now, in bed with Helene,
the natural light of reason makes known
to me what is to be known. So I say
"Helene! You are a pure spirit. You represent
truths such that they bear their evidence
on their face. As for me, I visit the butcher
to watch the slaughtering of cattle. There

I dissect the heads of the animals
to learn what imagination consists of."
—Francine lies beside me in her box. But
whether she sleeps or wakes I don't know.
"Francine ! Here are my dreams. Pay attention,
Francine/machine The world is light, light-rays.
Love is a theory of light which intends light."
I know what I am for. But do I exist?

Although nothing imagined is true,
the power of imagining is real.
Certainly I *seem* to see. I seem
to hear. I seem to be warmed. To imagine
is nothing other than to contemplate
the image of a corporeal thing.
That is what you must assure me of. What
you are for. But you do not assure me.

THREE

"WARBLE," SAYS THE BIRD

"Warble," says the bird. "Waters are many."
"Warble," says the bird. "The light is one."
On the waters the light skips and prances,
but the east *is* the face to which we turn.

Wounded, wound, draped and thrown
over the thin scum of persons, living and dead,
is a low cloud of thought, birdsong in
the half-dark at the end of our time,

and, over that, the sower's scattering hand,
or the arc of the sower's shovel swinging low
above the threshing floor of ocean
where the seed reaches its end, and stops.

"Warble," says the bird. "Earth is not the only green.
The scum is green between the air and rock.
I say the east is a face to which I turn,
but sun without color is not the sun."

THE FAMISHED DEAD

To this bloody pit—my heart—they crowd.
They drink my blood.
That way they become visible—*aware*—
and speak.
"Open that bloody pit."
"Look!" I reply,
"I have other plans!"
"In fact," Death says, "you've nothing else
to do."
They block the stair and quarrel
among themselves. I tell them,
"The rule is *one at a time*."
But whenever *anybody* is let in
the rest utter heartbroken cries. . . .

*

Now, here is Louis, my father. He comes
to remind me how
he once sold 500 new cars in one year.
I say to him, "Louis, I wish I'd known."
—"Would that have made a difference, Allen?"
"I think it would have, Louis."
—"I had a hard time getting here, Allen.
But *that* makes it worthwhile.
How'd I sell those 500?—Without shifting gears
I drove each customer—in reverse—up a steep hill.
The rich live up there in the light and air."

*

And here comes Ilona Karmel, the writer,
dead and buried
among *goyim* in Mount Auburn cemetary.
They dropped a big rock on her coffin before
they filled up the grave—so she wouldn't
walk anymore.
But, even alive, she had a hard time
walking, because the right side of her body
was run over by a tank when the camp
was opened at the liberation. She wrote
two books: *Stephania* and *An Estate of Memory.*

*

Farmer Herrmann says, "Heh! Allen,
it's been raining
for weeks. Come on! We've *got* to worm
the sheep."
Sheep are stupid. Hermann talks only to goats.
If Hermann has something to say
to the sheep,
any goat will get it across for him.
I, too, talk only to goats. In my dream
I say, "Hermann, what're you doing *with no goat?*
I learned from your goats. Your goats taught me something
about the dreaming sheep. You taught me nothing."

*

And now
into my dream comes a fragrant tree,
a frequent visitor. A lady reigns up there.
In the huge lower branches
is her throne.

Beneath the tree is a table. Here the Lord rests.
Sit down with me, you, whoever you are.
Breathe. Breathe in the fragrance beyond all fragrances.
Sit and eat and drink your fill in the shade.
You, too. Drink her blood in this shadow, from
time to time – from month to bloody month.

*

The last time I met my old girlfriend,
Emunah (the name means "faith")
was in a Jerusalem supermarket.
She'd married an archivist, one of
the twin sons of Schocken, the publisher.
She doesn't know her husband's name because
he doesn't know which twin he is.
At night
he fakes pages missing from old Hebrew books
by soaking xeroxes in tea—while his absurd
wife guards Jerusalem with an M16.

*

Now look! That other shadow is Pat, my
old nurse.
She had no body even then. She wore what
nurses wore *instead of bodies* in those days.
That's why her being dead now makes no difference
to me. What's important is still her body.
"Take it off, Pat.
Instead of breasts to suck, you wore two pins.
Instead of a cunt, God knows what you had there.
I am alive still, and passionate to know
for sure,
dear ghost, that what I miss you never were."

*

Every Sunday afternoon
my grandfather, Harry
Berman, now dead but formerly living on
Plymouth Avenue, Minneapolis—
the North side—
visited Pope Pius in Rome. As a matter of courtesy
Harry did so on Sunday, because Sunday,
as Harry understood the matter, was
a day off for popes. On each of these occasions
Harry said, "*Gut Yontiff, Pontiff.*"
And the Pope
replied to Harry – as one poet to another—
"*Was ist neues, Pius?*"

*

In my dreams I also see an unborn infant,
abandoned, unnamed, never to be named
in a desert of the unborn I know of,
never to be planted and never harvested,
forever yet to be. The infant is
silent. But I hear it. I say what it says.
I don't omit a syllable. The language
of the unborn is my language. Take note!
These words are words of a man unborn.

*

All night long, under my window, a dog
is biting a bone. Will the dog be done
when the moon sets? Will the dog be done
ever? —Not in the dark of the moon will
the dog be done. Not in the light of the sun.

Also, moonlight does not stop the sound,
the sound of the bone-biting dog. And we
know very well daylight does not stop it.
—Therefore, I give you the morning star.

TREASON

No more. I'm at the end of all of it.
"Allen, what is it like to be at the end?"
I am (strange but true) like a treasonous
feather falling from under the wing of
a startled bird that rises suddenly,
in alarm, off the branch of a gray birch
(short-lived tree, in any case) because someone
is walking along the path.

               "What is the history
Of feather-fall?"

             —Whenever you say something
considered, you also say: god is what
founds the dignity of human substance.

Therefore, poetry is a rigorous science,
because it is a path of the considering one.

Summer
is gone.

The falling feather is what cannot be thought about.
It is noticed or unnoticed. It is the very thing
without a name. If it grieves, there is no consolation.
If it draws the mind, there is no keeping of it in mind.
It is quickly forgotten.

The considering one must continue and does.

Whatever he sees, nothing he sees counts as reason
to stop.

A KISS FOR YOU

Somebody taught me this,
fifty years ago: "Everything in an unknown
way of being is unknown. If there is a city,
that city has no name—call it what you will.
If there is a language, that language doesn't
name anything,
whatever you may think. Even if there is rain
day after day, nothing grows in the streets
of Chicago." Then she said, "Take this kiss.
You are *mine* forever."

A GUST OF WIND

A gust of wind has blown the window open.
Where in the world is the scene of instruction?
Is it a mountain top? Is it a bed?
Or this long road down which we walk together,
the two of us—well acquainted. But also

strange to one another who, nonetheless,
are going the same way for a few miles
with the expectation of parting soon
without disappointment at a place we both
know of. ("You! Look *there!*" "And you also! *There!*")

"We *two?*"—More than two? Perhaps. But not fewer.
Two at least. Each one correcting the direction
of attention of the other: "Look there."
"There?" "Yes! Yes! Yes!—*Nothing is known to one.*
That mountain not. That bed not. This long road *not.*"

A gust of wind has blown the window open.
Look! Out there the apple tree is barren now.
The season has changed. Soon something will happen.
But *where* are you? Missing. Oh! *When last seen?*
—Now, cold rain. After that, silent in darkness, snow:

Where in the world is the scene of instruction?
In the Roman army, a soldier who has served
his time becomes a veteran, *exempt,*
and goes to fight afar. Before, there was
little time. And now there's no time at all.

FOUR

LOST, LOST

from the Autumn Collection
(Vogue, August 1957)

Look! There she stands in four-inch heels, posing
for her picture—*finesse.* She's the god's pleasure
("like ours, at its best, for short moments"—as
Aristotle says, *Metaphysics* XII, vii, 9).
Her body lights the sea-road to Port Sunlight—
imperial seat of soap ("Sunlight Soap"):
glimpse, glimpse, glimpse, glimpse, glimpse.
Behind her, and to her left, is a boy.

He is stooping to pick up a stone. Nothing
about him is right—e.g., his necktie is astray. . . .
He will wander on—*lost, lost*—always at night,
among the dead on State St. in Chicago.
They're strangely dressed, the dead on State.
"Comrades!" he says. And the dead say, "Comrade!"
Then the dead talk on: "The world does not come
from that which is not." "Nothing moves itself."

"The mover is desire. Look, kid! The eternal
moves without being moved. But, in Chicago,
matter is not going to set itself in motion.
Its movement depends on a motive cause
—*finesse. And there she stands*—posing for her picture:
slim, *gamine,* with toque, clutch bag, and Vareuse
dress by Fredrica.—The world does not come
from night, or from 'everything being together.' "

Whatever the mind—that nameless sage who utters
poems of the mind—says, it says out loud

all the way to the end of the dictation,
and is always saying out loud to each sleeper
and is heard by no one other than you
(and also, *remember*, by everyone else on earth).
"What does it say now?"—"It's going to snow."
"It is already snowing in the light."

MY RADIANT EYE

Or is it on account of my radiant eye
I have lived so long?— I never slept

in the study hall, or called anyone
by an improper name. I never urinated in

a desolate synagogue. I never ate or drank
in a desolate synagogue or picked my teeth.

I did not walk into a desolate synagogue
in the summer just because of the heat,

nor in winter just because of cold rain.
Also, I know one may not deliver a eulogy

for an *individual* inside a desolate synagogue.
But you can read scripture inside a desolate

synagogue, or you can teach in a desolate
synagogue, or deliver eulogies for the community.

When synagogues are deserted they are
 to be left alone and weeds allowed to grow.

One should not pick the weeds, lest there be
anguish that the synagogue is in ruins.

When are the synagogues to be swept
so that weeds do not grow inside them?

When they are in use.—When synagogues are
in ruins, weeds are not to be picked there.

Because I know these things I was approved,
although unworthy, after a three-day oral

examination before the king of Sicily
to whom by custom the power of approval

is entrusted. Thereafter, I have worn the
laurel crown—my eye radiant to this day.

RAIN ON A STILL POND

She's come.—Suddenly the room where I sit
feels emptier than before. If I look up now,
I will see her standing in the open door
gazing in toward me with her question.
And I am less because she's here, not more.

It is as when, on a summer afternoon,
raindrops begin to fall in utter silence
on a still pond. And a canoeist out there
lifts up his eyes and sees, looking at
the water, how water is falling into water.

A new solitude, until that moment
not known—it is the empty universe
of her voice—passes into my heart,
like water vanishing into water. She says,
"When you return to the shore, canoeist,

and are rested from your journey, remember me.
Among the histories of rain I linger to hear,
I linger to hear your answer to my question:
How do you merit to live so long?"
Then I say to her: "*Dilectissima*, it is as when

the sky darkens imperceptibly and a wind
moves slowly, as great things do, high up in
trees at the shore, not yet touching the surface
of the still pond. And then one raindrop falls
on the still water, without sound, and makes a circle.

First one drop falls and makes a circle. Then
another, at a distance. The first circle is
larger than the second at the moment of
the appearance of the second, and lingers.
Then the pond is stricken by a third raindrop.

The second circle grows large. But the first
raindrop of the shower has disappeared.
A big wind descends upon the pond.
Time is told telling of our lives, each of us
appearing and disappearing." Once more

I hear her question. Or is it the wind.
"But how do you merit to live so long?"
And then she vanishes, water into water.
Turning from the door I sit alone
once more. But this time taught, as by a daughter.

ABIDE WITH ME. FAST FALLS THE EVENTIDE....

The sybil with raving lips utters words, utters joyless things,
unbedizened, unperfumed, that reach across a thousand years
thanks to the god in her.

O Kid! Come to the window.—"What's there tonight?"
Now, in the altered light, not a breath.
All flesh is grass and mowers are in the field.
The harvest is lifted up and stored,
making the mow more empty than before.

The facts are subject to a new control.
The sparrows shriek: "O."—Desperate
sparrows trapped, in the dark, by an iron roof.
Beyond the fields, the land slopes down and falls
from this ledge, through the city, to the water's edge.

At hand, the schoolhouse interrupts the light.
Study the school: its tower clock and bells utter
quarters, halves, and hours.

                    I have made poems,
and written them down fifty years and got
just this far. Now, they talk only of war.
At midnight it snows across a thousand years.
Study the school. That sybil heard by all
utters joyless words, thanks to the god in her.

PORT SUNLIGHT

Once more I dream. A voice says:
"Build a house for the sun, with a winding stair
for the wandering light to go up and
rest before labor.

Cold, cold are the winds from the unmade world.

                    —Summon the mighty
trades: shipwrights, pipe-fitters, naked foundrymen,
and lens grinders—(all of them philosophers)—
and also the secret masons, and the garrulous
watermen (to pass the time on long crossings).
Let the name of the house be Port Sunlight."

Cold, cold are the winds from the unmade world.

Who will wake the sun in his well-built house,
Port Sunlight? In this room, curtains are drawn
and the window-shades are down. The shades knock
against the frame of the open window. Winds
live and die in the garden. The garden oak,
in its mysterious well, puts questions:

    "The clock—what does it say?
    The scales—what do they weigh?"

Cold, cold are the winds from the unmade world.

Between sleeping and waking, one afternoon,
the sun hears sounds downstairs and dreams of bodies,

mysterious actions and couplings.
Suddenly, the sun hears something *unmistakable*:
Beatrice—*in heels*—is coming up the stair.

Cold, cold are the winds from the unmade world.

—This is the last song you will hear from me,
the masterwork that comes to mind at the
final moment, when it is too dark to see . . .

VOCATION THE THIRD DREAM

Better the thoughts of one man alone. Many
cannot know the whole.
The whole of knowledge is known only by
the solitary thinker. When am I alone?
Not ever. . . . Only in death . . . which is coming

FIVE

HOW THE IMMENSE CATHEDRAL FELL

"How *did* it fall?"—It was so empty. So silent.
Everything *fell*. At first, the falling bricks
from somewhere dark, high up, out of sight.
One, and then several. Not many at once.
But nothing struck the ground. *Then* many.
Then all. Then nothing. Then the same materials
appeared again as another immense
cathedral—empty, silent, made of the
same bricks. But this time also many dark limbs
came down, as if the horror of materials,
the waste (the fatal repudiation, negligent
endangerment) was of bodies.—At first
slow, out of the darkness. Then, inevitable,
utter ruin. ("*Solomon*! What *was* your trade?")
I woke paralyzed by the terror of loss,
unable to move. Alive but stricken. Ignorant.
—So that's how the immense cathedral fell.
It was so empty. So silent! Everything fell.
"But now light increases. The dead bury the dead."

THE SUN DOES NOT BEGIN THE DAY

When does the day begin? When does the day end?
The sun does not begin the day. What does begin the day?
The call wakes us. If there is no call, no waking.
If there is no waking, there is no day.

Let me not sleep on.—Waking is daily.
Day after day someone says to everyone:
"You have slept enough." Each day dies in sleep.
Let me always hear the call: "You have slept."

But, in fact, the sun does not wake everyone. . . .
Consider all the sleepers who, despite the sun,
every day sleep on and on. Consider
also the wakeful in the dark, excruciate

from the beginning of the world, for whom
waking is beyond endurance. Let there be no call
to lengthen the pain of the sleepless. . . .
But the call comes still to those for whom waking

is beyond endurance. Also to young
men from whom rage has taken away all hope.
The voice is indifferent. Even when the sun
no longer rises and sets, the voice will wake

some who rise willingly, and leave others
in agony long after. The day begins
in sunless cells. The sun rises and the
day begins also in the grave.

And it does not end when there is no hearing.
It does not end when there is no light. Where,
where in the world have they built that burning church
made of wood cut in hills around and about the sun?

AT SUNSET

Now the sun sets and all the ways grow dark.
Persistant warble of a bird at my window,
in the dark. March 18, 2001—
my conviction of my own death. ("Get ready!")

Beginning with someone else's death, a word,
and ending with the other death, my own,
the first word of the next life is "death,"
and the last word of this one is not yet

thought upon. But elegy is the song.
Teacher, do not set enigmatic tasks.

THE BLACK TOWER

I raise
my eyes.
I am still
at sea. . . .
But now
on the
horizon
the ocean
thrusts up
a black tower.
The cook
is catching
birds.—An
old song:
All life
death ends.
And each day
dies with
sleep.

SPLENDOR

The eye altering alters the world.
Alters all.
"Come here, Josephina.
Help me thread the needle.
There will be wedding.
Six bridesmaids and twelve groomsmen
need splendor."

VOTRE ALTESSE

(a letter)

Elizabeth, my first student, *your highness*
to whom I owe all the joy of my life,
I am now in the service of Christina,
the queen of Sweden. I write to tell you
about the queen, *whom I will not outlive.*

She is my *last* student. Recognize her.
She is death. Death and dismemberment.
Please remember it was not the subject of
the instruction but the hour of the meeting
that killed me. She commanded me to rise

at 4:30 AM to meet her coach, I who
am accustomed to rise late. She read our text,
"The Passions of the Soul," on horseback while hunting.
We know the seat of the passions is not
in the heart. But remember, your highness, Descartes.

THE TITLE OF THIS BOOK CALLED

Descartes' Loneliness

The "Descartes," in the title of this book of poems, is a *meditating* philosopher—not just one name in the history of philosophy, but a name which stands for all persons insofar as we— you and I, *each one of us alone*—discover the world for the first time and, therefore, must think (*each one of us must do so alone*, there is no other way) as if no one had ever thought about the world before. It is this person who writes *poetry* and for whom it is written.

Our human life is distinguished from other life by language. Poetry is the ancient artistic form of language, our distinction. We, each one of us alone, think in our solitude about our *own* mind and about the world, in language—and each finds out thought about the self, about other persons and their claims upon the self, speaking and answering, by means of language. For the poets of my generation, the example of Cartesian meditation may be taken as definitive. Thus *Descartes' Loneliness begins* with the composition of a time and place ("Toward evening, the natural light becomes / intelligent and answers, without demur / "*Be assured ! You are not alone. . . .*"). In this time and place composed, I find a person. And thus he begins to speak, for *speaking* is the way given to us—and poetry is nothing less than speaking in the space of encounter, you for example with me—always when we think about it, always alone. And I with you. In the practice of speaking, the poet finds the world of persons, and by reason of the fact that there is a world of persons, each alone, who speak what he does, what poets do.

Poets are persons aware of aloneness and *competent to speak in the space of solitude*—who, by speaking alone, make possible for themselves and others *the being of persons,* in which all the value of the human world is found. *But never assuredly—* never without the saying of it (it does not "go without saying"), which saying is what the poet can do, if he is any good at all.

—But, at the end of this book you have in hand, the best this poet can say to you, and the most he can ask of you, is this: "We know the seat of the passions is not / in the heart. But remember, your highness, Descartes!"

—ALLEN GROSSMAN

THE ETHER DOME
AND OTHER POEMS: NEW AND SELECTED 1979–1991

In *The Ether Dome,* Allen Grossman gives his readers a retrospective of a life in poetry that has brought him such honors as a Guggenheim Fellowship, the Witter Bynner Prize of the American Academy and Institute of Arts and Letters, and a MacArthur Fellowship. Richard Howard has written: "A powerful poet, a vigorous and inclusive critic, Allen Grossman is undeterred by the tong wars of our literary establishment."

$10.95 US / 978-0-8112-1177-2

THE PHILOSOPHER'S WINDOW
AND OTHER POEMS

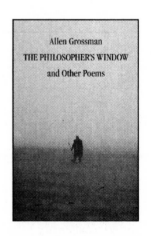

The speaker in these poems, Allen Grossman tells us, is "an old man compelled by the insistent questioning of the children to *explain* himself"—and in this way, the world. He begins with creation ("The Great Work Farm Elegy"), recalls the romantic quest of youth ("The Philosopher's Window"), and returns to reality ("The Snowfall"). His tales told, the old man wakes in a stormy springtime, "when the lilacs are gone." Grossman's allegory of life's journey, at once sonorous and antic, takes in the high and the low in these visionary songs of innocence and experience.

$12.95 US / 978-0-8112-1300-4

HOW TO DO THINGS WITH TEARS

How to Do Things with Tears, "the master-work of Allen Grossman's poetic life" (Jorie Graham) is a book brought forth by the "Sighted Singer." "This is a HOW-TO book," Grossman explains. "The heroic singer of tradition is blind. A NEW singer in this present must be sighted. In this book the poet intends to say something, insofar as a poet can, about the common sadness of living and dying in the world." Like the blind bard of old, Grossman's Sighted Singer conjures visions that evoke the sorrows and laughter of the gods and men.

$14.95 / 978-0-8112-1464-3

SWEET YOUTH:
POEMS BY A YOUNG MAN AND AN OLD MAN OLD AND NEW (1953-2001)

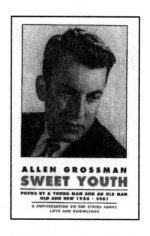

Robert Fitzgerald once wrote on Allen Grossman's early work: "At times they seem poems of a great age, poems at the world's verge, at the verge of time." The poems of the Sweet Youth, some of them dating to the early '50s, were original-ly collected in the poet's first three books: *A Harlot's Hire* (1961), *The Recluse* (1965), *And the Dew Lay All Night upon My Branch* (1973). Since then, there have been various books of poetry and prose, though in *Sweet Youth*, all the poems of the Old Man are new, written in Grossman's seventieth year.

$18.95 / 978-0-8112-1522-0

Please see our website (www.ndpublishing.com)
for a complete listing of titles by Allen Grossman